A Pictorial History of
REVIVAL

To all those who have kept the flame burning in Wales 1904–2004, people like the

Rev T. Hywel Jones (Emyr's father).

A Pictorial History of
REVIVAL

THE OUTBREAK OF THE 1904 WELSH AWAKENING

KEVIN ADAMS & EMYR JONES

BROADMAN
& HOLMAN
PUBLISHERS

Nashville, Tennessee

0-8054-3194-2

Dewey Decimal Classification: 269.24
Subject Heading: REVIVALS \ RELIGIOUS AWAKENING—WALES

Published by Broadman & Holman Publishers
Nashville, Tennessee

Published in 2004 in Great Britain by CWR under the same title

1 2 3 4 5 6 7 8 9 10 10 09 08 07 06 05 04

Contents

Foreword

One picture," it has been said, "is worth a thousand words." Never has that statement been truer than in this pictorial history of Welsh revivals—with a special focus on the revival of 1904–1905 under Evan Roberts—put together by Kevin Adams and Emyr Jones.

As a child brought up in Wales, I heard much about the revivals of the past from the preachers who came to the little village church that my parents attended. I would listen, enthralled, to stories of such great revivalists as Christmas Evans, Daniel Rowland, Thomas Charles, Hywel Harris, William Williams, and, of course, Evan Roberts. It was a thrill to open the pages of this pictorial history and see the faces of these great men and women of the past and, in some instances, to see the church buildings where they conducted their powerful ministries.

One has only to look at the faces of those who were used by God in the revivals of Welsh history to see etched there their passion after God, their deep commitment to His Word, and their longing to see men and women enter the eternal kingdom.

We owe Kevin and Emyr a great debt of gratitude for their painstaking research and the way in which they have put together a brief history of the outstanding moments in Welsh religious history.

As I said in the foreword to its sister publication, *A Diary of Revival*, my hope and prayer is that while you are perusing this book, the Holy Spirit will touch your heart, as He has touched mine, with a passionate desire to see God move, as history shows He is able to move, in great revival power.

Selwyn Hughes
LIFE PRESIDENT
Crusade for World Revival (CWR)

Introduction

A century ago Wales experienced a powerful religious revival that not only impacted the Church and Chapel culture of the day but also made front page headlines all over the world. Evan Roberts the most prominent of the revivalists soon became a household name, his methods and message being imitated throughout the Principality. Much was written at the time chronicling the extraordinary events – full chapels, powerful preachers, dramatic conversions and changed lives. Although much of this information is still available to the researcher it remains out of print and hard to access for the general reader much of it still untranslated from the Welsh language. Something similar can be said concerning a visual history of the time. For most readers names remain without faces and places associated with the main events products of their own imagination. This book seeks to add something of that visual dimension to this spiritual story.

Beginning with an overview of the spiritual history of Wales the book seeks to illustrate the story of the revival by using contemporary photographs of the people and places involved. Alongside these use has been made of modern images that help place the incidents in their proper historical context.

As this book is a companion volume to *A Diary of Revival ... The outbreak of the 1904 Revival* it does not aim to tell the whole story in detail but rather to add a more visual dimension to the one told in that book and others on the history of the movement. Our hope is that those who are already acquainted with the story will at least find something new and unique in this publication while those who are newcomers to it will be encouraged to find out much more.

One hundred years later as Christians celebrate and give thanks for what was accomplished by God through the churches at the beginning of the last century it is a temptation for many to indulge in bouts of spiritual nostalgia while waiting passively for God to do it again in Wales. It is not the purpose of this work to seek to encourage such attitudes. The Wales of then is not the Wales of now, things have changed and not just the fashions but society itself. The Christian influence of chapel and church is now something which is on the periphery of Welsh culture so different from its position in the years immediately preceding the revival of 1904 when it seemed to be so central with its popular preaching services and its numerous well attended mid-week meetings. A recognition that we still have a long way to go will guard over-enthusiastic optimists from unreal expectations and spiritual disappointment. A reversal of the present situation will not be a magic overnight affair, rather it will be an on-going battle to win back Kingdom ground, a battle that will not bypass the Church and Christians of this generation but will intimately involve them in the struggle, a struggle both private and public for God's perfect will to be done on earth as it is in heaven.

This pictorial history is the story of how a number of believers incarnated that will into their own lives and became living visible images of God's desire for the rest of the nation. Before dreaming of the blessing of another visitation the Church must wake up to the challenge of bending itself to that same Divine will and in so doing strengthening itself for the task ahead. Our prayer is that this volume in some small way might once again envision believers to be actors not just spectators in God's present purpose for His people.

Map of Wales

Anglesey

Bangor ●

Caernarfon ●

Bala ●

New Quay ●
Blaenannerch ●
Cardigan ●   ● Newcastle Emlyn
Nevern ●

St David's ●

Carmarthen ●   Dowlais ●

Llanelli ●
Loughor ●
St Govan's ●

Cardiff ●

Mae hen wlad fy nhadau

annwyl i mi / Gwlad beirdd

a chantorion enwogion o fri

/ Ein gwrol rhyfelwyr

gwladgarwyr tra mad / Dros

ryddyd collasant eu gwlad

1

Wales –
Land of Revival

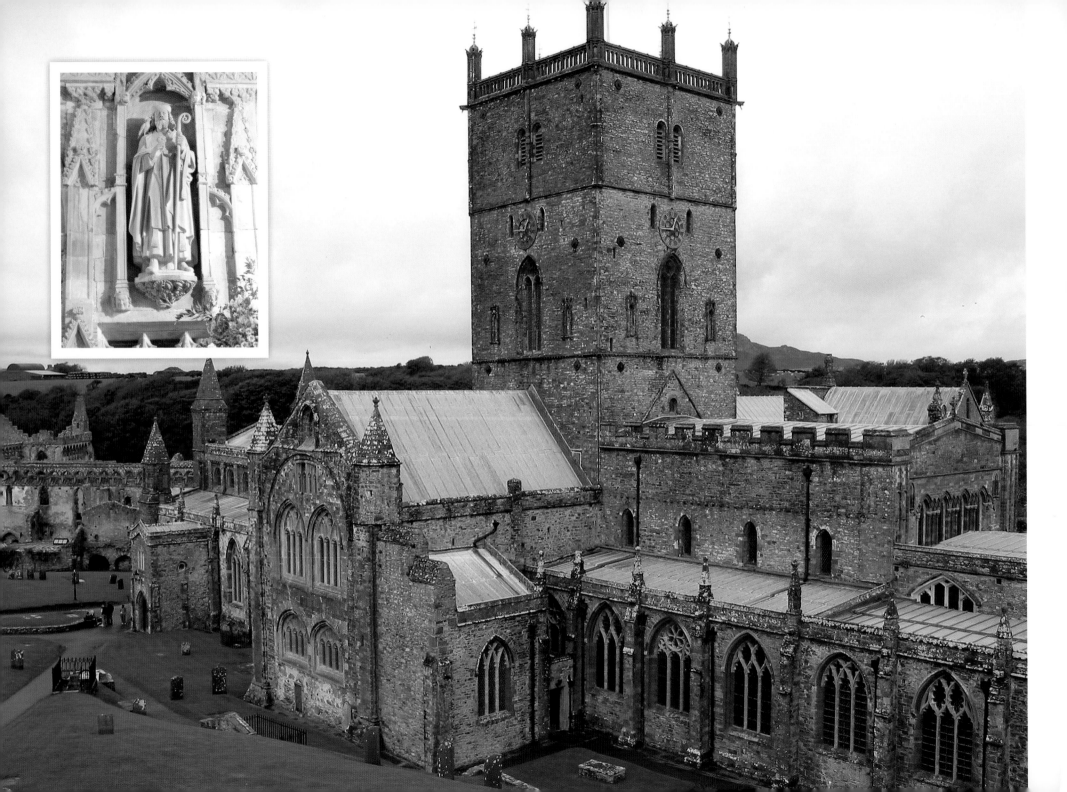

< St Govan's.

Most of the early churches in Wales were built of wood and have not survived. St Govan's, although probably built in early medieval times, captures something of a pre-Norman feel with its architectural simplicity and strong positioning on the Pembrokeshire cliffs. Its closeness to the sea reminds us also of the Celtic missionaries' zeal to travel in order to spread the good news. ∨

< St David's Cathedral is a medieval building erected on an early Celtic Christian site dating back to the sixth century. These monastic missionaries were the earliest successful preachers of the gospel to the native Welsh. The cathedral is named after Wales' patron saint, St David or Dewi in Welsh.

< Detail

Although churches from Celtic times have
not survived the ravages of time, there are
still many Celtic crosses dating as far back
as the seventh century in Wales. These are
often beautifully carved and symbolise some
of the key elements in Christian teaching.

Cenarth Falls in Carmarthenshire –
Some scenes in rural Wales have remained
unchanged since medieval times.

REMAINS OF THE CLOISTERS OF MARGAM ABBEY.

GLAMORGANSHIRE.

The sixteenth-century Reformation was not taken
on board spiritually by the Welsh people – it was
too much akin to a foreign import – yet, like the
rest of the United Kingdom, the changes brought
about by the Reformation meant a change in the
landscape of Welsh society with the dissolution
of the monasteries which had so coloured Welsh
medieval life. The ruins of this medieval legacy
are still to be seen throughout the land.

< Engraving of remains of Margam Abbey

Henry VIII **>**

Henry VIII's Reformation became far more
evangelical under his successor Edward VI.
Yet this was short lived, and after Edward's
death, Queen Mary sought to re-establish
Catholicism. Wales, which was little affected
by Henry's changes, was similarly less
affected by Mary's turning of the tables.
Although there were nearly 300 deaths
throughout the kingdom, only two of these
were in Wales.

Elizabeth I reintroduced the Protestant faith.
It was during her reign in 1588 that the
Bible was translated into Welsh.

MERTHYRDOD Y DR FARRAR,

YN NHREF CAERFYRDDIN,

MAWRTH 30TH 1555.

< The martyrdom of
Bishop Farrar at
Carmarthen,
30 March 1555

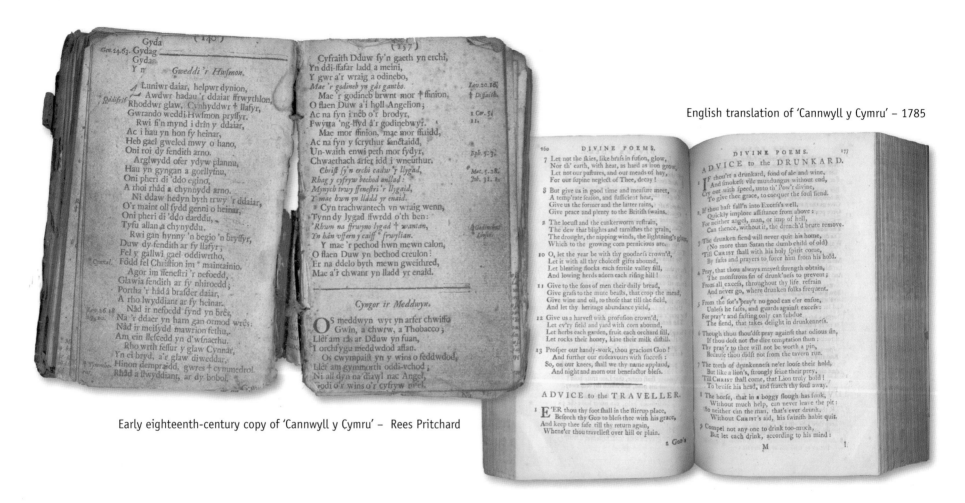

English translation of 'Cannwyll y Cymru' – 1785

Early eighteenth-century copy of 'Cannwyll y Cymru' – Rees Pritchard

The seventeenth century saw some spiritual advances in the land under the influence of the Puritans who sought by preaching and teaching to purify the Church. Some eventually took their stand outside the established church of that time while others worked conscientiously within. Of these, the most well known is Rees Pritchard of Llandovery, who put the Message in rhyme so that the ordinary layman might remember the Message. A collection of these was published after his death by an enthusiastic Welsh Puritan, Stephen Hughes. These evangelical and moral verses, summing up truth in a concise and memorable way, again helped to awaken the Welsh to a more spiritual religion.

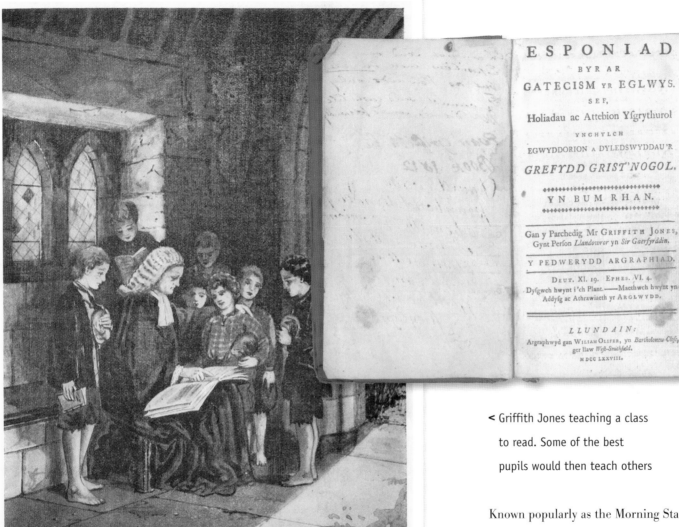

Griffith Jones teaching boys to read.

< One of Griffith Jones'
catechisms outlining Christian
teaching

< Griffith Jones teaching a class
to read. Some of the best
pupils would then teach others

Known popularly as the Morning Star of the eighteenth-century revival, Griffith Jones an Anglican clergyman set up Circulating Schools to teach the mainly illiterate population, using the Welsh Bible as a text book. The Welsh slowly began to understand the message of Christianity – both mentally and spiritually. The Bible which had been translated into Welsh nearly 150 years previously was now beginning to be translated into the lives of ordinary Welsh people.

Hywel Harris ∧

A year of Beginnings

Daniel Rowland >

∨ William Williams

∧ George Whitefield

1735 was a key date in the development of Welsh Christianity with the conversion of the zealous and determined Hywel Harris who travelled the country spreading the good news of the Christian gospel. At the same time, and independent of him, a clergyman called Daniel Rowland was also converted and became another key teacher of evangelical truth in eighteenth-century Wales. This was also the year of George Whitefield's conversion and the three soon became acquainted. This was the dawn of the Methodist revival, a revival that was to change the shape and feel of Welsh Christianity. It was also a revival that gave the Welsh its hymnology through William Williams, the Welsh Charles Wesley. Many of these hymns are still popular today – one of the most well known being 'Guide me O Thou Great Jehovah'.

Thomas Charles >

v Christmas Evans

PARCH. WILLIAMS O'R WERN.

^ Williams From The Wern

By the beginning of the nineteenth century, the Methodist Awakening had influenced the other two key denominations. The Baptists and Congregationalists now had their own Revival preachers and leaders – Christmas Evans for the Baptists and Williams from the Wern for the Congregationalists. These soon became the spiritual heroes of the growing Welsh Nonconformist population.

< John Elias preaching

v John Elias

Preaching became a key feature of Welsh worship and thousands flocked to the big meetings to hear the Bible explained. John Elias who in a few years would become a star attraction spoke of the time he attended the great meetings at Bala at the end of the eighteenth century. He recalls the first time he attended the great meetings as a 19-year-old in 1792.

He and a group of young people walked 40 miles there and 40 miles back, to hear the great preachers of the day. As they walked they sang psalms and hymns – while others took part in prayer. The conversation was all about the Bible and preaching – while the ministry was full of power and life.

See *Hunangofiant John Elias*, GP Owen. EMW 1974 pages 56, 57

Bethania Baptist Chapel, Morfa, Llanelli

As the nineteenth century wore on chapels began to proliferate throughout Wales as more and more people responded to the Christian message. By the second half of the nineteenth century, chapel building was at its height, while older buildings were regularly extended and modernised to cater for the increase in demand.

Map showing growth of >
denominations in 1830

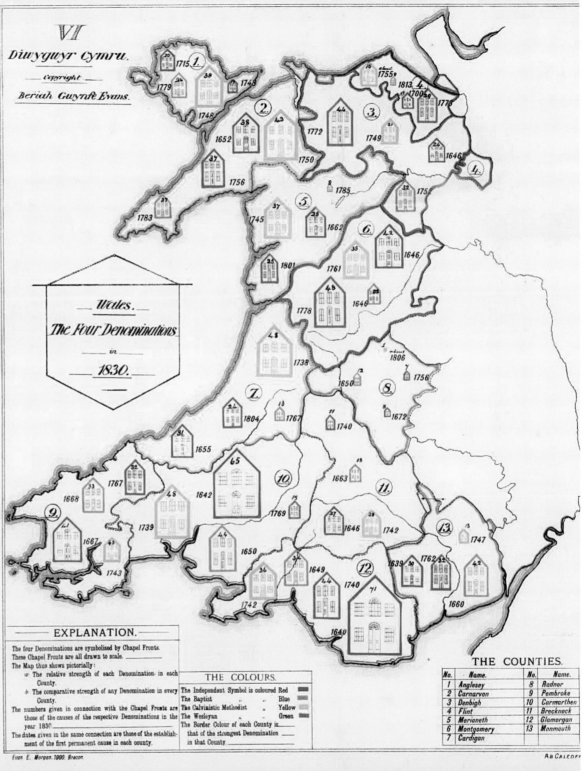

VI

Diwygwyr Cymru.

— copyright —

Beriah Gwynfe Evans.

Wales.
The Four Denominations
in
1830.

— EXPLANATION. —

The four Denominations are symbolised by Chapel Fronts.
These Chapel Fronts are all drawn to scale.
The Map thus shows pictorially
  a The relative strength of each Denomination in each County.
  b The comparative strength of any Denomination in every County.
The numbers given in connection with the Chapel Fronts are those of the causes of the respective Denominations in the year 1830.
The dates given in the same connection are those of the establishment of the first permanent cause in each county.

THE COLOURS.

The Independent Symbol is coloured Red
The Baptist   „   Blue
The Calvinistic Methodist „ Yellow
The Wesleyan   „   Green
The Border Colour of each County is
  that of the strongest Denomination
  in that County.

Evan E. Morgan. 1900. Brecon.

R.B. CALEDF?

THE COUNTIES.

No.	Name.	No.	Name.
1	Anglesey	8	Radnor
2	Carnarvon	9	Pembroke
3	Denbigh	10	Carmarthen
4	Flint	11	Brecknock
5	Merioneth	12	Glamorgan
6	Montgomery	13	Monmouth
7	Cardigan		

∧ Maesyronnen Chapel. Oldest Nonconformist Chapel in Wales, circa 1690s.

Park Street Congregational >

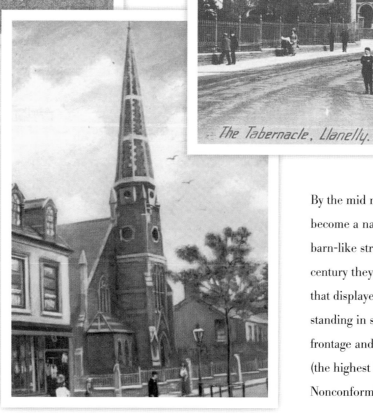

The Tabernacle, Llanelly.

By the mid nineteenth century Wales had become a nation of chapels. From the simple barn-like structures of the early nineteenth century they developed architectural styles that displayed their growing confidence and standing in society. Tabernacle's classical frontage and Park Street Chapel's steeple (the highest in Llanelli) are examples of Nonconformists' increasing strength.

Bethlehem Congregational Chapel, Pwlltrap Nr St Clears

The steady growth of Nonconformist Christianity is illustrated in the numerous dates adorning the chapels of the land.

Built 1765

Renewed 1909

Expanded 1785

Seats put in 1871

Renewed 1833

DAFYDD MORGAN.

< David Morgan

< Humphrey Jones

1859 Revival

1859 was the year of the great national revival in Wales and other parts of the United Kingdom. It arrived from America through Humphrey Jones and throughout the next year and a half spread throughout Wales. It was estimated that 100,000 people were added to the churches – its most well known leader being David Morgan.

The Rev J. Cynddylan Jones >

Cynddylan Jones was a well known author, biblical commentator, theologian and preacher who championed orthodox and evangelical teaching within his own (Calvinistic Methodist) and other denominations. During the 1904 Awakening he helped provide a sound historical context to the whole concept of revival in Wales.

v David Adams

PARCH. DAVID ADAMS B.A.

Photo. by H. J. R. Wills, Cardiff.

Y Parch. J. CYNDDYLAN JONES, D.D., Whitchurch.
GANWYD: Capel Dewi, Ceredigion, 1841.

By the end of the nineteenth century Welsh Christianity was beginning to feel the influence of the higher liberal criticism of the Bible. Someone who popularised this modern liberal approach was David Adams, a Congregational minister, who sought to make distinctions between the teaching of Paul and Jesus. This was eventually to lead to a 'social gospel' as it became known in the early twentieth century. Yet although liberalism had made some in-roads, popular Nonconformity was more or less orthodox in tone and belief.

Fedra i iddim dweyd llawer
heddyw: ond yr wyf fi yn caru
Jesu Grist o waelod ynghalon
—fe fu farw drosta i / Fedra
i iddim dweyd llawer heddyw
ond yr wyf fi yn caru Jesu

2

Dawn of
Revival

< The Rev W.S. Jones who returned from America to Penuel Baptist Chapel, Carmarthen.

< W.W. Lewis – Minister of Seion Chapel, Calvinistic Methodist, Carmarthen.

∨ Penuel Chapel, Carmarthen

Keri Evans – Minister of Priory Street Congregational >

W.S. Jones is regarded by some as the forerunner or torch bearer of the revival. Returning from the States in the late 1890s, he brought with him a fresh passion and zeal for revival and renewal in Wales.

R.B. Jones wrote of him: 'It was at once observed that the minister who had returned to Wales was different from the one who had left Wales a few years before. "You must be born again" in those days seemed a strange text for a popular preacher …'
Rent Heavens p26. R.B. Jones 1930

The town of Carmarthen soon became a spiritual hot spot in the months preceding the national outbreak in November 1904.

Carmarthen Castle ∨

The Rev F.B. Meyer – a key speaker of the First Keswick in Wales Convention. **>**

THE REV. F. B. MEYER, B.A.

During the summer of 1903 at the first Keswick in Wales Convention at Llandrindod, a number of young ministers convicted of their lack of spiritual power, gave themselves to the Lord. These fired-up young men went back to their churches and sought to spread their new-found zeal. These again were the beginnings of a new work in Wales.

R.B. Jones writes of his experience 'This power has been given me to overcome numerous temptations. Oh how sweet it is to pray! What a wonderful book the Bible has become! … In consequence of myself – surrender to Him, I am His and He is mine.' Letter to a friend. 1903 (Rupert Ellis, *Living Echoes*, p43 Delyn Press)

R.B. Jones **>**

Commemorative plaque at St
David's to Dean Howell   >

Dean Howell's article which appeared in
December 1902 was later regarded by
many as prophetic of the nearing spiritual
awakening …

'What is Wales' greatest need? … There
has never before been so much preaching,
but what of the effects? … Take note, if
this was to be my last message to my fellow
countrymen … before I am taken to the
Judgement it would remain thus … The
greatest need of my dear nation and country
at this time is spiritual revival through a
specific outpouring of the Holy Spirit …'
Y Cyfaill Eglwysig, December 1902

Dean Howell died just a few weeks after the
article was published, his last message to his
nation immortalised by its fulfilment.

DEAN HOWELL.   [*To face p.* 104

REV. SETH JOSHUA,

Mission Diary 1904

JAN 1	My one strong desire is to live out the consecrated life during 1904.
MAR 27	I have prayed for 50 conversions.
28	The fifty souls were made up.
APR 12	Numbers are under conviction. They hold out with stubborn determination. I cannot remember seeing such resistance to God's power. If it breaks I think there will be a blessed revival!
JUL 22	I find that my prayer life is becoming deeper and more consistent.
SEP 18	There is a remarkable revival spirit here. I have never seen the power of the Holy Spirit so powerfully manifested among the people as at this place just now. (New Quay)
19	The revival is breaking out here in greater power. Many souls are receiving full assurance of salvation. The spirit of prayer and testimony is falling in a marvellous manner. The young are receiving the greatest measure of blessing. They break out into prayer, praise, testimony and exhortation in a wonderful way. (New Quay)
NOV 18	Sophia Gardens Field (Cardiff). This path alongside the River Taff has become sacred to me. I have seen the Hawthorns blossom three years in succession and fade again as I have prayed along its shady path. I have wrestled for personal baptism of the Spirit and for a national revival. It has come and I rejoice.

Ref – Seth Joshua. Diary CMA Mss 17916 National Library of Wales.

Harbour at New Quay

TABERNACLE CALVINISTIC METHODIST CHURCH, NEW QUAY,
In which the Revival Originated. (Photo by D. O. Jones, N

REV. JOSEPH JENKINS,

∧ Maude Davies and Florrie

– two of the New Quay Youth

The Reverend Joseph Jenkins had been for some months concerned about the low state of spirituality in the churches of his area. He set about organising conventions to remedy the situation. The first being held on 31 December 1903 and 1 January 1904. His challenging message eventually began to effect the youth of his church. Seeking a deeper commitment a Miss Florrie Evans asked his advice – he responded by asking her if Jesus was Lord over all her life. On the second Sunday of February 1904 in the youth meeting following the Sunday morning service Florrie Evans stood up to testify that she loved the Lord Jesus with all her heart. These words became the spark that ignited the revival fires. Fires that eventually would spread throughout Wales. These Spirit-filled, enthusiastic youth were to meet with Evan Roberts some six months later at Blaenannerch.

Florrie Evans

May Phillips

'*I am unable to say very much today but I love the Lord Jesus with all my heart – he died for me.*'

2nd Sunday February 1904 (note date)

Testimony and Prayer

'Do you know that I was tired of life?
Time was tiresome to me – it wore me out
– thinking of eternity was out of the question
– But thanks be to God I now know what I
will do with eternity!'

'Give me truthfulness, Give me purity,
Give me honesty. You are Clean, Pure and
Truthful – The Truth itself – You are the
Truth – You are all the Truth! I am overcome
by You O God of Truth!'

Florrie Evans

Testimony and Prayer

'I have been unable to pray for months.
Everything seemed so hard: but since last
night I can pray as much as I want – the door
is open wide …'

'Thank you for mercy: mercy to a great sinner
like myself. Thank you that you are a Great
Saviour. Make me clean, make me pure. You
cannot make me bigger – I'm only small.
Make me pure – radiant – a little radiant
shining pearl in your magnificent crown.'

May Phillips

Tabernacle, New Quay

Plyg fi! Plyg fi! Plyg ni!

Oh Lord Bend me / Plyg fi!

Plyg fi! Plyg ni! Oh Lord

Bend me / Plyg fi! Plyg fi!

Plyg ni! Oh Lord Bend me

/ Plyg fi! Plyg fi! Plyg ni!

3

The Story of
Evan Roberts

Parents & Upbringing

Mr. HENRY ROBERTS
(Tad Mr. Evan Roberts).

< Evan Roberts at 26

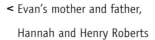

< Evan's mother and father,
Hannah and Henry Roberts

< Island House

Island House or Temperance Villa situated just a few hundred yards away from the Loughor estuary where Evan swam and played during his childhood.

Born in 1878, Roberts was brought up in a typically Welsh religious home where attendance at chapel on Sunday and mid-week was obligatory.

The Story of Evan Roberts 47

LOUGHOR BRIDGE.

E.M.J.

< The bridge of the
Loughor Estuary

Evan lived at Loughor for most of his early
life, only moving from there at the end of
the Revival.

< Modern Loughor

Miners filling a tram ∧

THE OLDEST AND YOUNGEST IN THE COL

∨ Underground scene

Similar to many other boys of his generation Evan left school before the age of 12 in order to help his father who had recently had a leg injury. He began his work in the mine by looking after the pumps moving on later to be a 'door boy' opening and closing the underground doors for the trams to pass. He narrowly escaped serious injury when a tram broke loose and nearly hit him.

PIT-TOP AND HEAD-GEAR

CLANNY SAFETY LAMP   DAVY LAMP   BELGIAN MUESELER
SAFETY LAMP

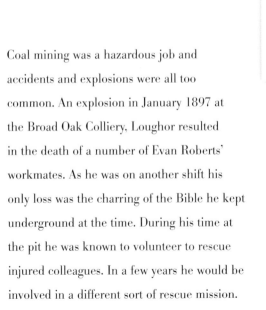

THE RESCUE AT GILFACH GOCH

Coal mining was a hazardous job and accidents and explosions were all too common. An explosion in January 1897 at the Broad Oak Colliery, Loughor resulted in the death of a number of Evan Roberts' workmates. As he was on another shift his only loss was the charring of the Bible he kept underground at the time. During his time at the pit he was known to volunteer to rescue injured colleagues. In a few years he would be involved in a different sort of rescue mission.

'Evan Roberts spoke of three books that greatly contributed to his spiritual development, besides the Bible. These included Thomas Charles' *Christian Instructor (Hyfforddwr) A Summary of Christian Teaching*, *The Welsh Calvinistic Methodist Hymnbook* and *The Pilgrim's Progress.*'

D.M. Phillips. *Evan Roberts*, pp. 65,66

Other publications in Evan Roberts' library included:

In His Steps – What Would Jesus Do? – C.M. Sheldon
Theological Dictionary – Thomas Charles
Outlines of Theology – A.A. Hodge
Ellicott's Commentary
Poetical Words of Islwyn
Numbers of bound periodicals
Welsh Encyclopaedia

D.M. Phillips. *Evan Roberts*, pp. 53,54

The spiritual journey undertaken by Bunyan's Christian in *Pilgrim's Progress* was one that Evan who, like Bunyan, had a vivid imagination himself, could easily associate with. Beginning with his conversion at 13 years old he too battled with the temptations of his time and felt the reality of the battle with Satan. This he expressed when speaking of his visionary experiences while at Newcastle Emlyn.

Christian's Journey in *Pilgrim's Progress*

Christian setting out.   Evangelist.   Slough of Despond.   Worldly Wise-man.   Interpreter's Gate.   Picture.

Passion & Patience.   The Fire.   Palace.   The Man of Despair.   Christian at the Cross.   Simple &c. asleep.   Formalist & Hypocrisy.   The Spring.   The Arbour.

Christian passing the Lions.   The Study.   The Armoury.   Fight with Apollyon.   Valley of the Shadow of Death.   Vanity Fair.   Trial.

Faithful at the Stake.   Chariot waiting for Faithful.   Demas at the Hill Lucre.   Lots Wife.   Discovered by Giant Despair.   The Dungeon.   Escape.

The Delectable Mountains.   Mount Clear.   Pilgrims in the Net.   Vineyards.   Crossing the River.   Celestial City.

< Moriah as it was during Evan's childhood and teenage years. The new chapel was built alongside the old in 1898. The old chapel then becoming the schoolroom in 1903.

Evan was one of 14 children, 8 of whom were still alive during the Revival.
The Roberts' boys. Left to right:
A younger brother (probably died before the Revival), Dan, David (Eldest), Evan >

Pisgah, Evan Roberts' Sunday school >

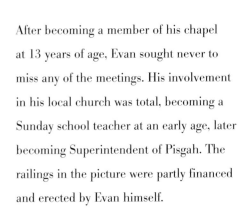

After becoming a member of his chapel at 13 years of age, Evan sought never to miss any of the meetings. His involvement in his local church was total, becoming a Sunday school teacher at an early age, later becoming Superintendent of Pisgah. The railings in the picture were partly financed and erected by Evan himself.

Leaving the coal mine in 1902, Evan became an apprentice blacksmith to his uncle and for the time of the apprenticeship lodged with him at the house next door to the forge. It was during his time at the forge that he finally decided to train for full-time Christian ministry.

Warned by his mother that this would be a hard life he replied 'I am willing to work for my Redeemer till my dying day …'

The forest forge today

Interior, Moriah Chapel >

Throughout the first few months of 1904,
Evan Roberts prepared to train for the
Christian ministry, preaching in local chapels
and passing denominational exams. He was
accepted as a candidate by his denomination.

Moriah Chapel in 1905 >

Trefecca College ∨

MARKET HOUSE, NEWCASTLE, EMLYN.

Newcastle Emlyn at the turn of the twentieth century

Sydney Evans ∨

In order to prepare for further study at Trefecca College Evan went to the Grammar School in Newcastle Emlyn on 13 September 1904 staying there about six weeks. His studies included English, History and Maths.

A personal friend and a fellow student at the school, Sydney Evans was to share in many of Evan's spiritual experiences during the months of September and October 1904. At the outbreak of the Revival he became another key revival leader and led meetings throughout Wales. He later married Evan's sister Mary and they both went to India as missionaries.

< Ty Llwyd, Evan and Sydney's lodgings at Newcastle Emlyn as it is today. It was in the garden of this house that Evan saw many of his visions.

< Evan Phillips during the 1859 Revival

< Evan Phillips and his wife

Evan Phillips had been the Calvinistic Methodist minister at Newcastle Emlyn for 40 years. He was well respected and well liked. He was his own man, loved to smoke a pipe, was interested in train spotting and never preached over 20 minutes. His down-to-earth attitude was one appreciated by all the students at the Grammar School.

Bethel Chapel, Newcastle Emyln, where Evan Phillips was minister

Sunny Side, Evan Phillips' home.

As it is today >

SUNNY SIDE

The family at Sunny Side

Back Row – left to right
Doctor Tom Phillips;
Magdalene; David; Rachel; Mary;
Isaac o Bersia (visitor); Margaret; Mrs Tom
Phillips; John Phillips

Front Row – left to right
Mrs Phillips; Ieuan Phillips; Rev Evan
Phillips; Anne Phillips

The family at Sunny Side were to be eyewitnesses of Evan's spiritual development during his time at the school. The girls Rachel, Anne and Maggie became close friends to Evan – sometimes worried, sometimes amazed at what they were witnessing.

Blaenannerch Chapel

The Manse at Blaenannerch

< Seth Joshua

Timetable
Thursday 29th September

6am   Evan leaves Newcastle Emlyn on horse-drawn cart with Seth Joshua and other students.

7am   1st Meeting of the day at the chapel with W.W. Lewis. In this meeting Evan hears Seth's prayer 'Bend us, Oh Lord'.

8am   Breakfast at the manse. Evan feels that God is offering him the Spirit.

9am   2nd Meeting – An open meeting where any who felt led might pray. It was at 9.30 in this meeting that Evan prayed the prayer that had been on his heart since the 7 o'clock service. 'Bend me, Oh Lord'. It was here that he received the Power.

< Evan Roberts with Bible

< The seat where Evan was filled with the
Spirit at Blaenannerch Chapel.

Following the Blaenannerch experience,
Evan Roberts was consumed with a passion
to evangelise Wales and during the month
of October sought God's guidance as to how
he should achieve this. It was during this
time that he experienced most of his visions,
confirming to him that God was about to
descend in Revival power.

After Blaenannerch, Evan wrote to a friend:
'I have received three great blessings
1. I have lost all nervousness.
2. I can sing all day
3. What an easy thing it is to give thanks
now.'

Newcastle Emlyn in October

< Capel Drindod

v Twrgwyn

Sydney Evans >

The Blaenannerch experience of September was followed by a month of searching for God's leading as to how to evangelise Wales. Evan prayed much about the possibility of a team to accompany him in a nation-wide mission and spent much time immersed in the Bible. His college studies suffered as all his time, energy and passion were being poured into this desire for spiritual revival. During this time he was involved in some local 'revival' meetings, led by Joseph Jenkins and the New Quay young people. These had a lasting impact on Evan and as the Revival itself progressed later in the year he would use many of the methods he had seen at Twrgwyn and Capel Drindod.

On Sunday 30 October, while listening to Evan Phillips preach, Evan Roberts feels God calling him to go back to Loughor — 'to take the plunge!' ...

< Evan Roberts and Revivalists re-visit Evan
    Phillips, March 1905.

Back Row

    D.J. Evans; Dan Jones; David Jones;

    Williams, Gethsemane; W.E. Williams;

    W.S. Evans; W.D. Davies

Second Row

    Mary Roberts; Jones, Ynys Hir; E. Williams,

    y-Gard; Rachel Phillips; Mary Davies;

    Magdalene Phillips

Third Row

    Sal Jones, Nantymoel; Sidney Evans;

    Evan Phillips; Evan Roberts

Front Row

    John Phillips; Maggie Davies, Maesteg;

    Annie Davies, Maesteg; Anne Phillips;

    S. Gwnfe Jones

Evan Roberts returned to stay with Evan
Phillips in March 1905 and during his
stay he revisited places associated with the
initial blessing including Newcastle Emlyn
and Blaenannerch. He took long walks with
friends seeking to rest and prepare himself
for the coming mission in Liverpool
(29 March –17 April 1905).

Dyma Gariad fel y moroedd
/ tosturiaethau fel y lli /
T'wysog bywyd'n bywyd n
/ Pwy - all beidio a chofi
andano? / Pwy all beidi
a thraethu i alod? / Dyma

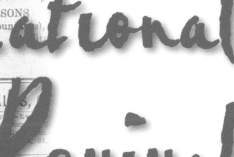
HOTEL SERVANTS.

WANTED, good strong General; reference required.—Apply Homfray Arms, Pill, Newport. e112

WANTED, a smart Married Couple (used to the trade), without encumbrance, to Manage Hotel; ry district; doing good trade; partly commercial. ad application, with age, references, and terms ired, to F 49, Evening Express, Cardiff. c2280

YOUNG Lady desires Engagement in first-class Bar; could assist in Bookkeeping if required; good nces.—Please address W., 40, Clive-street, Cardiff. e3758110

BARMAID.—Required, young Lady, with experience and good references.—Apply to Manager, Sandring- Hotel, St. Mary-street, Cardiff. e3757110

WANTED, Cook-General.—Apply Hotel Victoria, Corporation-road, Newport, Mon. c3748110

RE-Engagement as Barmaid; colliery district pre- ferred; disengaged 12th January.—F 46, Evening ress, Cardiff. e3690111

WANTED, a sharp Girl as Useful Help in business house; used to children; willing to assist in when required.—Apply, stating wages required, to hes Hotel, Quay Parade, Swansea. e3688111

WANTED, Barmaid for colliery district; references required.—Apply J. Edwards, Queen's Hotel, mney. e3729112

WANTED, for Suburban Hotel, experienced Barman; references required.—Apply Tredegar Hotel, ath. e3869110

BARMAID wanted (experienced); used to a quick counter trade.—Apply, with photo and references, ite, Kimberley, Milford Haven. e3653319

NURSES.

NURSE wanted for Two Young Children; must be experienced; personal application preferred.—Mrs. amberlain, Bertram Hotel, Broadway, Roath. Cardiff. c2290

EXPERIENCED Nurse wanted; able to take entire charge of a Baby two months old.—Apply Mrs. E. Brown, Caroline-street, Bridgend. e3765110

ISCELLANEOUS SITUATIONS.

LL Servants Booked and Suited Free; Ladies' Booking 1s.—191, Chepstow-road, Newport. e111

WANTED immediately, Grocery Haulier; assist in Warehouse and help Bread Delivery; accustomed of horses. Apply with reference and stat.

PREMISES.

MESSRS S. HERN AND PERTWEE, AUCTIONEERS, VALUERS, SURVEYORS, HOUSE AND ESTATE AGENTS. For list of Business Premises and Houses to be Let or Sold see "Western Mail" daily. Printed Register free. Offices, 93, St. Mary-street, Cardiff. Established 1840.

WANTED, House at Pontnewydd, or in vicinity.— Apply R. S. Pugh, Blaenavon. e3646110

ELMSLEIGH, 126, Llandaff-road, to be Let or Sold; £400 can remain at 4½. e3737112

1, Wordsworth-avenue, and Offices adjoining; immediate possession can be given.—Apply on premises. e19

TO Let (Furnished), the Semi-detached Villa "Cae Parc," St. Helen's-road, Swansea; centrally situated; near trams, parks, and sands; possession February 13th, 1905.—John F. Harvey and Son, Auctioneers and Valuers, 3, 4, and 5, Goat-street, Swansea.

TO be Let, Hackerford House, near Llanishen; partly furnished or otherwise; with 25 Acres of excellent Land; good stables and buildings.—Apply Rev. W. Evans, Tregare, Raglan. c2231

THE Law of Landlord and Tenant; price 1s.; postage 2d.—Stationery Department, Western Mail, Cardiff.

OFFICES.

OFFICES to Let: commodious and well-lighted; most central part of Cardiff.—E. Nelson and Co., 3, St. John's-square. e15173

ST. Mary-street, Cardiff.—Several well-lighted rooms, singly or in suites, in Western Mail-chambers; electric lighting; lavatory on each floor.—Apply Mr. E. H. Crafter, Western Mail, Cardiff.

JAPANNED Tin Deed-box, with lock, to take fools- cap sheet; price 4s. 6d.—Stationery Department, Western Mail, Cardiff.

GOOD, English-made Black Lead Pencils, 5s. 6d. per gross; special value.—Stationery Department, Western Mail, Cardiff.

THREE very large rooms on ground floor, 1 St. Mary- street, Cardiff, suitable for solicitor, architect, auctioneer, estate agent, &c.; rent, £45.—Apply Mr. E. H. Crafter, Evening Express, Cardiff. e13005

TO Auctioneers and Others.—To Let, Suite of Rooms on ground floor, Western Mail-chambers; rent very moderate.—Apply Mr. E. H. Crafter, Evening Express, Cardiff. s13000

PUBLIC-HOUSES.

JEWELLERY FOR SALE.

LADY offers quite privately magnificent 10-guinea Service A1 Plate, comprising dozen each table, dessert spoons and forks, also teaspoons (80 pieces); unsoiled; accept 35s.; approval willingly.—F 22, Evening Express, Cardiff. e3655117

ENGAGEMENT Rings.—Fine Selection; exceptionally low prices.—Sol. Phillips, 43, Caroline-street, Cardiff.

WEDDING Rings; best value for money.—Sol. Phillips, Jeweller, 43, Caroline-street, Cardiff.

DIAMOND Rings (ladies or gents); big bargains; see windows.—Sol. Phillips, Caroline-street.

SIGNET Rings; in variety; initials or monogram gratis; useful gifts.—Sol. Phillips, Estab. 1850.

WATCHES, "Less than Cost"; over-stocked; big bargains.—Sol. Phillips, Pawnbroker & Jeweller.

CHAINS (ladies or gents); big bargains; see windows.—Sol. Phillips, 43, Caroline-street, Cardiff.

BROOCHES, in variety; useful presents; wonderfully cheap; see windows.—Sol. Phillips, Caroline-street.

SCARF Pins; now fashionable; very useful presents; bargains.—Sol. Phillips, Jeweller, Caroline-street.

BRACELETS (curb and others); special purchases; big bargains.—Sol. Phillips, Jeweller, Estab. 1850.

SILVER Plate, Clocks, and Ornaments; see our new show windows; marvellously cheap.—Sol. Phillips.

UMBRELLAS (ladies and gents); gold and silver mounted; best silk covers; call and inspect.

MUSICAL Instruments.—Violins, Banjos, Guitars, Mandolines, Concertinas; bargains.—Sol. Phillips.

IS your watch Wrong? The best and cheapest shop in Cardiff for the repair of watches of every description (English or Foreign) is 38, Castle Arcade (third shop from Castle-street), by James Keir (for ten years with Mr. Spiridion). Clocks and Music Boxes cleaned and repaired. e9171

MUSICAL.

PIANOS and Organs.— Dale, Forty, and Co.

"ANGELUS" Piano-player.— Sole agents, Dale, Forty, and Co.

"HUMANA" Piano-player; highest grade at a low price.— Sole agents, Dale, Forty, and Co.

MUSICAL Instruments of all kinds.— Dale, Forty, and Co.

PIANOS Tuned and Repaired.—Dale, Forty, and Co.

DALE, Forty, and Co., Piano and Organ Merchants, High-street, Cardiff. a514

"Evening Express" Circulation.

AUDITORS' CERTIFICATE.

Cardiff, 21st November, 1904.

We have examined the books of "Evening Express" and certify that the circulation exceeds

100,000 Copies per Day.

DAVID ROBERTS & SONS (Chartered Accountants).

MISCELLANEOUS SALES.

CROSS Brothers' Scale Department.—Ly Scales kept in stock; repairs low prices; send for illustrated Brothers, the Cardiff Ironmongers street.

NEW Year Gifts.—Rajah Ci each box of 50.—Nelson, Tobacco rdiff.

FRESH Herrings, 10s.; Box Bloate Reds, 2s.; Box Cured y, d.; Fish from 1s. stone; Small e, Co ake docks, from 1s. 4d. stone; ers, 4s. Salt Cod, 2s.—Frederick Lo Fish Merc Docks, Grimsby

CREDIT Drapery.—James Whitaker is still old well-known address, 1, Clare-gardens, side, Cardiff, and can give best value in Tailor Drapery. Specialities: Gentlemen's and Youth and Overcoats, ready made and bespoke; also Costumes, &c Write immediately for pattern

CHEAPEST House in South Wales for all Revolving Heels; extraordinarily cheap lines 2s 6d.; ladies' 1s. 3d. per dozen; hawkers and supplied.—47, Bridge-street, Cardiff.

Monday 31 October 1904

< Loughor Station

< Evan Roberts

On Monday 31 October 1904, Evan Roberts arrived home at Loughor convinced that God had called him to share his experience with the young people of his own chapel. He asked his minister for permission and when given he proceeded to start nightly meetings in Moriah and Pisgah.

Jack Lewis, Swansea

G.W.R. Disaster, Llanelly, Oct. 3rd, 1904.

Copyright

The same people who looked on in amazement at the railway disaster just outside Loughor would in a month be amazed at spiritual revival in their neighbourhood.

<< Mary Roberts, Evan's sister

Mary on the Revival team at Liverpool >

During the first week of services, Mary Roberts becomes a changed woman.

'My sister, a girl of 16, who before was a sarcastic peevish girl, has had a ground change, and her testimony is that she is happy now, and that there is some joy in living. You can see the change in her face.'

Letter to Elsie Phillips, Saturday 5 November 1904

∧ Mary later married Evan's best friend Sydney. They spent many years working on the mission field in India.

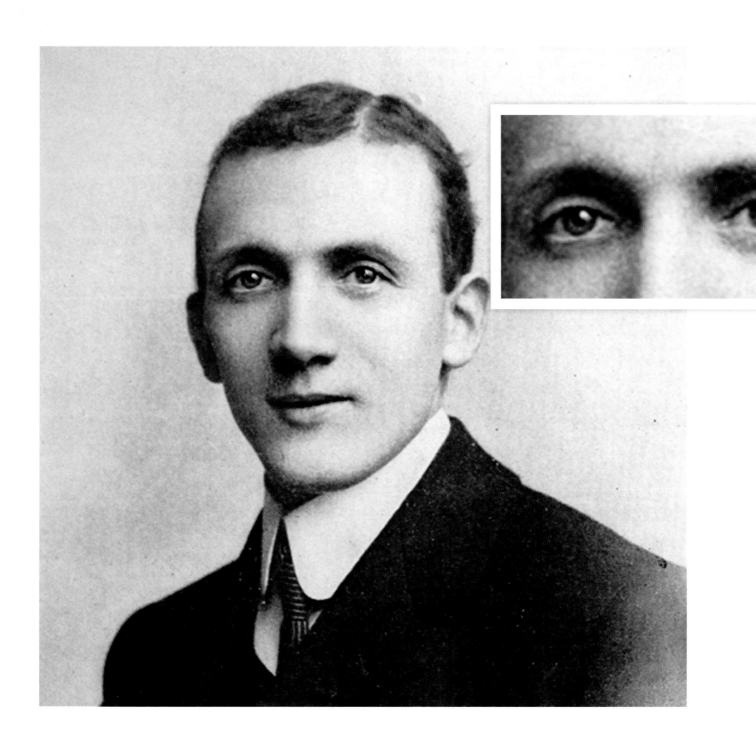

< Dan Roberts,
Evan's Brother

On Evan's arrival, Dan, Evan's brother, had just been informed that his sight was seriously deteriorating and was unable to work. On hearing this, Evan informed him that the Lord needed him and that his eyes would be healed. They immediately were and Dan went on to be a key Revivalist in the coming months. He never suffered with his eyes again.

It was in the Moriah vestry on Monday 31 October 1904 that Evan Roberts began his public Revival ministry.

Letter to Elsie Phillips Saturday 5 November 1904:

'We began this mission Monday night, and we hold a prayer meeting at eight pm. These meetings have been a success. The young people say that they could sit all night. Monday night I explained to them the object of the mission. ... and urged them to prepare for the Baptism of the Holy Spirit. Now this is the plan I have taken under guidance from the Holy Spirit:

1. If there is some sin or sins in the past not confessed, we cannot have the Spirit. Therefore we must search, and ask the Spirit to search us.

2. If there is something doubtful in our life it must be removed.

3. Total surrender to the Spirit. We must do and say all he asks us.

4. Public confession of Christ.

These are the four things leading us to the promised blessing. This is our success this week in public confession: – Monday night 16, Tuesday 6, Wednesday 4, Thursday 20, Friday 19 – Total 65'

Interior of Moriah Vestry

'The Holy Spirit led me to this place. He has blessed my mission abundantly'

Moriah Vestry >

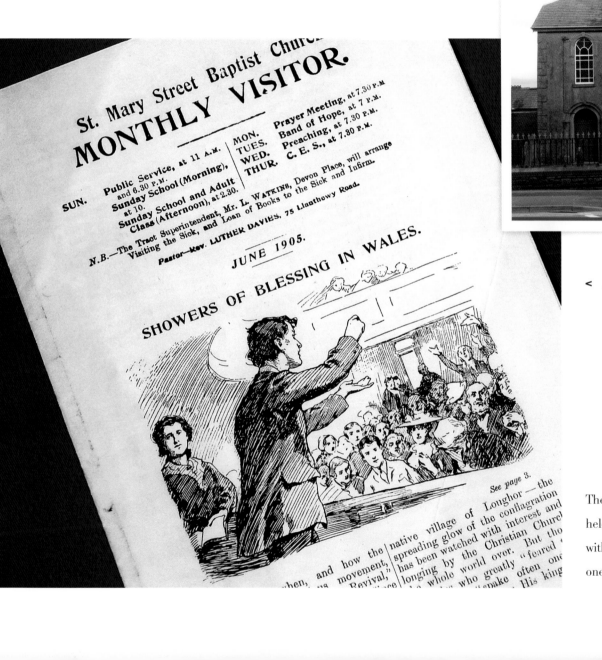

< A church newspaper of the time

The first Evan Roberts' Revival meeting was held on Monday night, 31 October 1904, with 17 adults including the Revivalist and one child present at Moriah Vestry.

'Prayer is the secret of Power'

Quote from Evans Diary

'Lord Jesus, help us now through the Holy Spirit to come face to face with the cross ... Put us all under the Blood ... We thank thee for the blood ... O open the heavens. Descend upon us now. Tear open our hearts – tear – give us such sight of Calvary that our hearts may be broken ... Open our hearts to receive the heart that bled for us ... Do what thou wilt with us. If we are to be fools – make us fools for Thee. Take us, spirit, soul and body. We are Thine ... Forbid that we should think what men say of us ... Amen and Amen.'

Prayer of Evan Roberts
Bangor, 24 April 1906

< Newspaper of the time
– Revival edition

News of the Revival was quickly spread throughout Wales and the rest of Britain by newspaper coverage. The message of the Revival was reported in detail by eye-witness journalists who inadvertently became carriers of the good news.

Newspapers described the meetings and reported on the number of converts gained in the various churches.

THE GREAT RELIGIOUS REVIVAL IN WALES.

The THIRD Part of the History of this Movement, from the columns of the "WESTERN MAIL" writt[en] [by] Special Correspondents, Illustrated with Portraits and Ske[tches]. 32 pages and cover, is Published TO-DAY (SATUR[DAY]) the 4th inst.

SOLD BY ALL NEWSAGEN[TS]

PRICE 1d., or by Post 1½d., from

WESTERN MAIL LIMITED, CARDI[FF]

The First & Second Parts may still be obtained at the sam[e].

REVIVAL SUCCESS.

JEALOUSY OF PREACHERS.

Evan Roberts's Charge.

A THREAT TO NAME THEM.

Liverpool Revival Scene.

A DRAMATIC ACCUSATION.

Service for Non-Adherents.

(FROM OUR SPECIAL CORRESPONDENT.)
LIVERPOOL, Saturday Night.

A special meeting exclusively for non-adherents is surely a novel feature even in a revival which, from its beginning, has been run on unusual lines. The idea of organising such a gathering was conceived in Liverpool, and to-night we witness in Liverpool the first attempt to carry the idea into practice. On paper the arrangements were perfect. Hundreds of pink tickets were distributed exclusively, so we were officially assured, to non-adherents, while canvassers who were responsible for bringing these "Esgeuluswyr" (backsliders) once more within hearing of the evangel, were supplied with white tickets, which secured their own admission, only on condition that they brought one or more non-adherents with them to the meeting. This is the first of three similar ticket meetings to be held

---

[...]ay from
[...] shortly
[...]he meet-
[...]pel was
[...]nnounced
[...] people
[...]g Aber-
[...]ogranog,
[...]hear the
[...]n. The
[...]s Llan-
[...]of being
[...]riosity.
[...]ee and
[...]greater
[...]issioner
[...]pulpit
[...]th him
[...]big seat
[...]nounced
[...]ip God
[...]y must
[...]r object
[...]e glory
[...]woman
[...]ance of
[...]d to be
[...]aviour.
[...] being
[...]in the
[...]ly two
[...]Roberts
[...]. stop.
[...]There
[...]oved,"
[...]mbers.
[...]be re-
[...]ed not
[...]or five
[...]simul-

A LLANBERIS MINISTER'S COMMENT.

The Rev. J. Evans Owen, of Llanberis, in this week's "Genedl Cymreig," states that a change has come over Mr Evan Roberts. What is the nature of the change he does not know. Dealing with the missioner's "future usefulness," he states :— "Unfortunately, instead of adhering to the writings of the New Testament, he has begun to associate with the Jewish prophets. . . . When the time comes for Mr Roberts to visit Liverpool he will be told by the Spirit not to go there. . . . It would be well if his friends would send him for a journey to Cannan, which would call his mind back to the present world. . . . It would be wiser to postpone his visit to North Wales. He deserves the sympathy and the earnest prayers of the whole of Wales."

THE REVIVAL AND TEMPERANCE.

Speaking at a conference of the South Wales section of the United Kingdom Alliance at Swansea on Thursday, the Chairman (Rev. J. H. Parry) said all who had come under the influence of the revival had of their own accord felt obliged to leave the public-house and take the pledge. The revival had in Llansamlet influenced some hundreds, and many of them, of their own accord, had taken the pledge. Many had told him that they felt it imperative to be total abstainers if they were going to be real followers of Christ. He believed the temperance question could not be separated from Christianity. Possibly in the past they had not taken the great care they ought at temperance meetings, not only to get people to sign the pledge, but to persuade them to become members of churches. Councillor C. F. Phillips said the revival had greatly helped the temperance cause.

GREAT WORK IN ABERDARE VALLEY.

There is no abatement of spiritual fervour in

A number of pamphlets were produced by the *Western Mail* by bringing together the main reports of Revival services.

The arrival of Mr. Evan Roberts and Party at Llanfairpwllgwyngyllgogerychwyrndrobwllsanttysiliogogogoch.

A SNAP-SHOT OF MR. EVAN ROBERTS.
In conversation with the Rev. John Williams, of Liverpool, on a road in Anglesey.

"MR EVAN ROBERTS" AT CEMAES

THE GREAT WELSH REVIVAL.   Mr. EVAN ROBERTS.

Much of what we know of Evan Roberts' thoughts at the outbreak of the Revival are contained in the many letters he wrote to

friends as the events were unfolding around him.

THE WELSH REVIVALISTS & FRIENDS.
✖ 1905. ✖

D. DAVIES, E. MORRIS, Miss J. EVANS, D. JONES, Miss M. DAVIES, PHYL JONES, W. JONES,
Miss MAGGIE JONES, Miss S. A. JONES, Miss MAGGIE DAVIES, Miss MARY DAVIES, Miss C. ROBERTS, J. O. MORRIS,
of Maerdy. of Nantymoel. of Maesteg. of Gorseinion. of Maerdy.

Some of the other Revivalists

< The Rev D.M. Phillips, Evan Roberts' first biographer was also a popular preacher in the Revival years

Y Parch. Dr D M PHILLIPS.

< The Rev J.T. Job, Bethesda, N. Wales

Evan Roberts was not the only Revivalist by any means. Many other men, including church ministers, were active in promoting the Revival. J.T. Job was active in North Wales and saw many added to the church.

Sam Jenkins, singer >

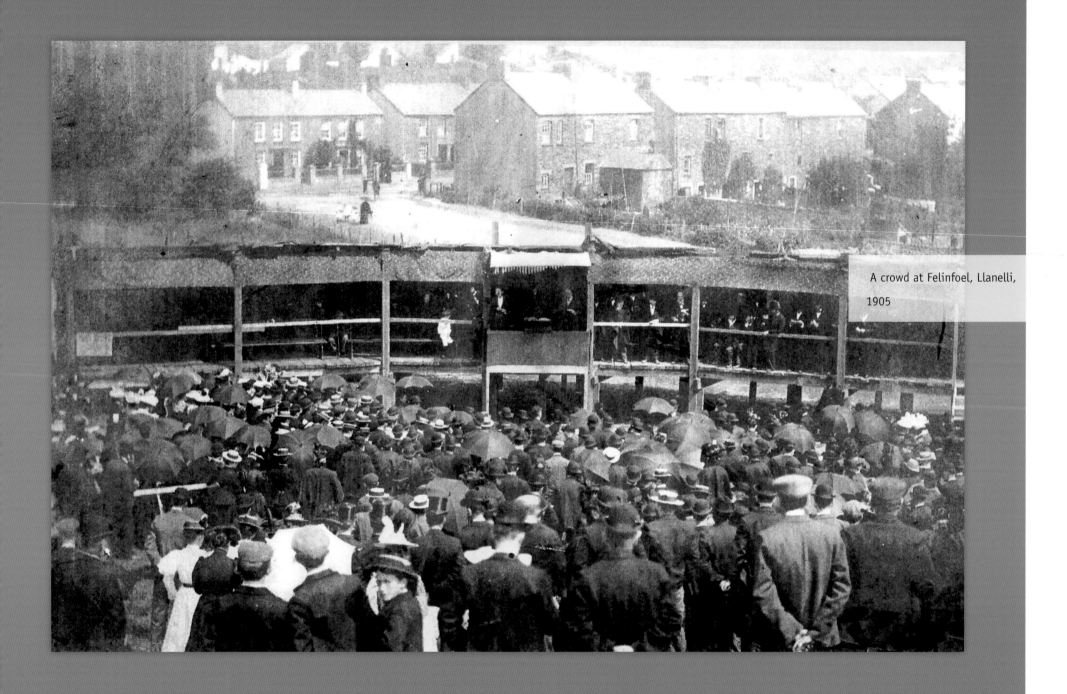

A crowd at Felinfoel, Llanelli, 1905

Mr. EVAN ROBERTS AND THE REVIVALISTS FROM LOUGHOR.

< Adverts for *Western Mail* postcards

^ Examples of *Western Mail* postcards >

Many postcards of Evan, his team and other Revivalists, were published early on in the Revival. The most well known were the series published by the *Western Mail*.

Mr. ROBERTS commenced his Mission by holding all-night Services at Moriah Methodist Chapel, Loughor. near Llanelly, on Nov 9th, 1904. Total number of Converts to March 31st, 1905 : 85,294.

Y GOLEUAD:

Newyddiadur Wythnosol.

PRIS CEINIOG.

CYNHWYSA y rhifynau am yr Wythnosau hyn Adroddiadau manwl am

Y DIWYGIAD

YN

NE A GOGLEDD CYMRU

gan liaws o weinidogion a lleygwyr.

Gyda'r rhifyn am IONAWR 13eg rhoddir

DARLUNIAU

o amryw o'r prif offerynau ynglyn a'r Diwygiad o'i gychwyniad

I'w gael trwy y post oddiwrth y cyhoeddwr,

E. W. EVANS, DOLGELLAU.

Y Lladmerydd.

Cyf. XXI.]   IONAWR, 1905.   [Rhif 240

Mr. Evan Roberts.

< Welsh religious periodical, *The Interpreter*

Evan Roberts preaching at Llanfachreth, 14 June 1905:

'The revivalist preaches at an open-air service in Anglesey, from the pulpit of the great John Elias, to 3,000 people.'

'The Lord be praised, the Spirit is at work tonight, and the enemy is fleeing covered with wounds, but there will be too many left if only one is unsaved.'

< A Revival postcard

Evan Roberts preaching in the open air in North Wales from John Elias' pulpit.

Mr. Wm. Venmore.   Miss Roberts. Rev. John Williams,   Mr. Hy. Jones   Miss Phillips
                                Sec.   Sec.

Dr. Phillips.   Miss Annie Davies.   Mr. Evan Roberts.   Mr. Wm. Evans,
                                                              Chairman.

Evan Roberts – Celebrity

< Newspaper cutting of the time

The Liverpool Campaign in the spring of 1905 was an organised mission with a committee of Liverpool church representatives. The venues were booked and organised beforehand, contrasting somewhat with the earlier missions of the Revivalists. Yet, though the meetings were organised, Evan seemed to remain, often controversially, his own man, determined to obey what he felt was the leading of the Spirit.

MR. EVAN ROBERTS, the Welsh Revivalist.
MR. DAVID LLOYD GEORGE, M.P. for Carnarvon District.
SIR ALFRED THOMAS.

Y Llun gan Haines.]

Y Gwir Anrhydeddus D. LLOYD GEORGE, A.S.
(CANGHELLOR Y TRYSORLYS),
Llywydd Undeb Bedyddwyr Cymru, 1908-09.

MR LLOYD GEORGE AND MR EVAN ROBERTS.

Our London Welsh correspondent writes :—
"Mr Lloyd George is the recipient of innumerable letters and telegrams of congratulation on his appointment as President of the Board of Trade. Amongst these communications not the least interesting was the one which he received from Mr Evan Roberts, the Welsh Revivalist, between whom and the President a very sincere friendship was struck some months ago. It will be remembered that in deference to the claims of the two revival meetings to be held at Carnarvon next week, Mr Lloyd George, with the concurrence of the chairman of the Welsh Parliamentary party (Sir Alfred Thomas) arranged for the postponement to the following week of the Welsh National Convention, which, it had been proposed to hold on the 28th instant. This consideration of the needs of the revival was received with great satisfaction, and he received the news, so said an informant, "with that indescribable gwên (smile) which is one of his chiefest charms." The gwen eventually broke out into poetry, and the following englyn, which has just reached Mr Lloyd George, was the result :—

"Lloyd George.
Ar fyr yn bybyr y bo—cei cwnau
Y "Cabinet" fflamio ;
"A! Lloyd George," meda ei Wlad o—cymeriad
Heb ball i'w gariad—Pwy eill ei guro !
E. R.

Accompanying the englyn was the following characteristic letter :—
Penygroes, Gogledd Cymru, Rhag. 12, 1905.
Anwyl Gyfaill,—Caniatewch i mi eich llongyfarch yn y llwyddiant presenol, yr hwn sydd yn anrhydedd fawr i chwi, a thrwy hyny yn wir anrhydedd i wlad boeth a chwir y Cymro. Doethineb y goruchaf fyddo i eich cadw a'ch codi yn y dyfodol. Hyn yn fyr mewn diolch a dymuniadau goreu.—Yr eiddoch "i godi y wlad."
Evan Roberts.

Mr Lloyd George, although he has never severed his connection with the little Baptist Church at Criccieth, of which his uncle, Mr Richard Lloyd, is the tower and strength, is whilst he is in London an active member of the Welsh Baptist Church at Castle-street, Oxford Circus. Last Sunday evening Mr Lloyd George, as he has frequently done in the past, delivered a short but impressive address on the religious aspect of national questions, and thanked the members of the church, who, on the proposal of Mr Price, supported by Mr John Hinds, had passed a vote of congratulation on his appointment, with the expression of an earnest desire that he may long be spared to aid and promote the principles of social and religious freedom.

Evan Roberts knew Lloyd George and Lloyd George knew Evan Roberts.

Lloyd George the MP for Caernarvon District showed a great interest in the Revival even cancelling political meetings so that they would not clash.

Duw mawr y rhyfeddodau
maith! Rhyfeddol yw pob
rhan o'th waith; Ond dwyfol
ras, mwy ryhfeddyw / Na'th
holl weithredoedd o bob rhyw!

5

Effects of Revival

Emotions often ran high in the Revival services as scores sought to respond in repentance and faith to the message.

'I didn't weep much in the Revival of 59 but I've wept lately till I'm weak yet amidst the greatest tears I have felt the greatest Joy'
Evan Phillips 1905

< A typical Revival scene

Evan Roberts comforts a penitent >

Singing

∧ William Rees, author of *Here is Love vast as the Ocean*

Evan Roberts favourite hymn, *Great God of Wonders* **>**

Revival postcard of one of the Revival hymns **>**

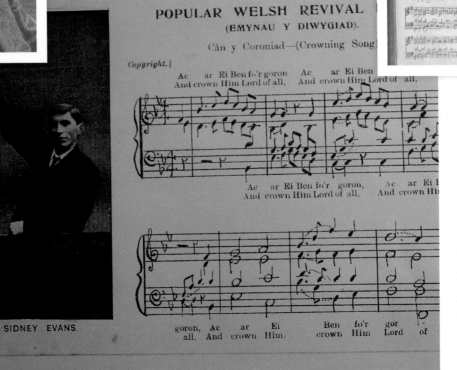

Spontaneous congregational singing without musical instruments became the norm in most Revival meetings as individuals sought to respond to the Revivalists' challenge to be instantly obedient to what the Spirit would tell them.

MISS ANNIE M. REES,
who was associated with Mr. Evan Roberts in the early
revival meetings and who led the revival wave in
Cardiff during December, 1904.

∧ Annie M. Rees

< The lady singers

Annie Davies became well known for her rendition of the great hymn 'Here is love vast as the ocean'. This often moved congregations to tears and it became known as the love song of the Welsh Revival. Annie Davies remained with Evan Roberts as his main soloist through the Revival, which led to rumours of their being engaged – rumours that sold papers but little else.

Here is Love
Vast as the
Ocean

Annie Davies, Maesteg

THREE OF MR. EVAN ROBERTS' LADY SIN

MISS S. A. JONES   MISS MAGGIE DAVIES   M
(M...)

< The singing sisters

For the first time women became prominent publicly in chapel meetings, singing and sharing their testimonies with the crowds. Although acceptable to most, this new innovation was too much for some.

A comic postcard of the period ˅

PEACE AT LAST

The years following the Revival saw the women again take a less public part in services. Public speaking, especially, became out of bounds as the professional male ministry once again ascended to their pulpits. It would not be till the latter part of the century that many women would feel as emancipated as in the Revival years.

REVIVAL HARVEST.

Returns Number Over 85,000.

The appended list of Revival converts, which shows a total of 85,294 has been compiled from returns furnished by correspondents throughout Wales. As the number of conversions is continually being added to, the list does not profess to be quite complete, but is as up-to-date as possible.

Aberaman	510	Llanelly, Loughor, and Felinfoel	1,756
Aberavon	325	Llanelly Hill (Brecon)	90
Aberbeeg	206	Llangattock	53
Abercarn	280	Llangeitho	45
Abercrave	83	Llangamnarch	20
Abercwmboy	156		

Newspaper cuttings of the day listing converts

...rdaman		Llanelly,	
...eravon	325	and Felinfoel	1,75...
...erbeeg	206	Llanelly Hill (Brecon)	
...bercarn	280	Llangattock	5...
...bercrave	83	Llangeitho	4...
...bercwmboy	156	Llangamnarch	2...
...bercynon	729	Llangennech	6...
...berdare	726	Llangyfelach	
...ergwynfi and Blaen-gwynfi	420	Llanharan	24...
		Llanhilleth	25...
...berkenfig	256	Llanishen	
...bernant	104	Llannon	2...
...bersychan, Pont-newynydd, Taly-waen, Garndiffaith, and Varteg	453	Llanstephan	
		Llawhaden (Pem.)	
		Llantwit Major	14...
...bertillery, Sixbells, and Cwmtillery	3,467	Llwydcoed	
		Llwynhendy	17...
...mmanford	220	Llwynpiod	
...arry	319	Maesteg and district	2,09...
...argoed	676	Maenclochog	
...eaufort	191	Maesycwmmer	15...
...edlinog	238	Maindee (Newport)	
...edwas	190	Mardy	66...
...ettws	50	Merthyr	94...
...irchgrove	15	Merthyr Vale	91...
...lackwood	38	Michaelstone	2...
...laenavon	368	Middle Hill (Haver-fordwest)	3...
...laengarw	1,290	Milford Haven	10...
...laenpennal	583	Miskin	1...
...laina	15	Morriston	1,86...
...ontnewydd (near St. Asaph)	1,069	Mountain Ash	1,03...
	15	Mynyddbach	1...
...recon	51	Nantymoel	3...
...ridgend	307	Nantyglo	56...
...riton Ferry	406	Narberth	
...ryncethin and District	145	Neath	1,3...
		Neath Abbey	
...rynmawr	486	Nelson	3...
...ryn (Port Talbot)	70	Newbridge	
...rynseion & Carvan (Pem.)	23	New Quay	
		Newport	1,...
...uilth Wells and district	216	New Tredegar	
		New Milford	
...urry Port	290	New Inn (Pontypool)	
...wlchyllan	30	Ogmore Vale	
...aerau	57	Pembrey and Pwll	
...aerphilly	570	Pembroke	
...apcoch	51	Pembroke Dock	
...ardiff	2,753	Penarth	
...ardigan and district	55	Penclawdd	
...armarthen	312	Pencoed	
...efncribbwr	75	Penderyn (Aberdare)	
...ilfrew and Coynant	122	Penrhiwceiber	
...ilfynydd	721	Penywaun (Aberdare)	
...lydach (Brecon)	70	Peterstone	
...lydach-on-Tawe	200	Pentyrch	
...lydach Vale	850	Penygraig	
...oedpoeth	70	Penyfae	
...oity	24	Pontardawe	
...owbridge	28	Pontardulais	
...oychurch, Treos, and Llangan	70	Pontlottyn	
		Pontnewydd	
...rickhowell	156	Pontrhydfendigaid	
		Pontrhydyfen	
...rosshands and Tumble	339	Pontrhydygroes	
...rosskeys	500	Pontyberem	
...rumlin	18	Pontyclun and district	
...rynant	85	Pontycymmer	
...wmaman	670	Pontygwaith	
...wmamman (Carm.)	559	Pontypool	
...wmavon (Port Talbot)	800	Pontypridd	1...
		Pontyrhyl	
...wmbach	402	Porth	
...wmbran	186	Porthcawl	
...wmdare	94	Pumpsaint (Car.)	

MODERN COLLIERS RETURNING FROM WORK

< Newspapers carried a number of cartoons depicting Revival scenes
– some positive, some negative.

< Coalminers 1904

< Illustration of an
underground prayer
meeting

'Employers tell me that the quality of work
the miners are putting in has improved.
Waste is less, men go to their daily toil with
a new spirit of gladness in their labour.'
(W.T. Stead)

The church truly went underground during
the Welsh Revival as miners expressed their
new found faith in prayer and praise during
their work breaks.

UNDERGROUND STABLES

< Underground pit ponies

'And I remember listening to the old ostler Evan Jones. I remember a fireman or deputy asking – "Well Jones how are you tonight Old Jones?"

"Oh David, Daniel David", said he, "I'm afraid of losing my job. I'm afraid of the boss getting to know I've nothing to do. I don't touch the animals for the boys look after them and clean and groom them and look after their gear and give them food and water – and I've got nothing to do ... I'm ... I'm afraid of the manager getting to know and I'm afraid of getting the sack." So he was weeping and the fireman said "Don't weep, according to the law we have to keep you here even if you don't do anything ... Is that not right Daniel?" ... "Yes. Oh I have been upset, I have been afraid of losing my job but the boys are singing and singing and they are kind to me and kind to the animals. It's wonderful because I have just nothing to do!"'

Witness of Mr Parell Parry (17/18 years old during Revival) Rhos – From Brynmar Jones Collection

< Contemporary comic postcard

v Cartoon from *Evening Express*

The social impact on individuals' lives was tremendous. While nobody could claim that they turned water into wine during the Revival, many demonstrated that they could turn beer into clothes for their children and food for their families.

THE LORD'S PRAYER.

"𝕷ead us not into
Temptation,
But deliver Us from Evil."

13

Public houses became targets for zealous converts who would hold open air services immediately in front of them, encouraging those inside to come out and join them on their way to the chapel. There were a number of occasions when the converts even 'invaded' the premises. Thousands responded positively and overnight became 'tee-total' in their new-found faith. This had the immediate effect of harming the beer trade whose sales in many areas decreased greatly.

< Civil unrest

'The Policemen tell me that the public houses are nearly empty, and the streets are quiet and swearing is rarely heard. It's easy for the Police here! – let them enjoy a blessed holiday I say. The area is happy to still employ them even for doing nothing!'
Witness of J.T. Job, Bethesda, N. Wales
3 December 1904

< Policemen at the beginning of the twentieth century

'Well the Revival is doing me good anyway?'
'In what way ?' asked my informant 'do you mean that you have more patients?'
'Not at all' was the reply 'but £23 due to me which was written off my books as hopelessly bad debts have been paid to me since the Revival began.' *Doctor's Testimony*

what has made the difference? (*See Page* 76)

MAGISTRATE: What? No cases! Another pair of white gloves for me. What's the meaning of it, sergeant?
COURT OFFICER: Revival, sir!

< *Western Mail* cartoon

Due to the Revival the crime rate went down as people were converted to be more honest and trustworthy. Many paid back old debts and a life of crime became a thing of the past, a social effect, which was felt throughout the land.

On New Year's Day 1905, 92 converts were baptised by the minister of Adularn Baptist church Felinfoel, Llanelli. It seemed the entire population of the village was present to witness the physically cold but spiritually warm proceedings. The converts' determination to brave the freezing waters was admirable only to be overshadowed by the minister's determination to personally baptize them all!

Llanelli Mercury 5 January 1905

Baptismal pool at Felinfoel, Llanelli

^ Contemporary postcard illustrating traditional church/chapel rivalry – much of which disappeared during the Revival years.

THE RIVALS
CHURCH & CHAPEL.

An Anglican eyewitness explains the Revival from his own perspective >

The Vicarage.
Pontarddulais R.S.O.
Feby 2nd 1905:

Dear Mr Mathias.

I am just recovering from a sharp attack of influenza, else I would have replied to yours sooner. With regard to the Revival in our parish and specially in the Church, I should like to say that we had experienced an indefinable something before we knew of the existence of Mr Evan Roberts. Some few weeks before Mr Evan Roberts began his meetings

in Loughor, some of my people
came to me and asked me & the
Clergy of this parish to conduct
a week's mission at Gorsenion,
& Pontardulais. And whilst I
was thinking about it, Mr Evan
Roberts appeared at Loughor.
Our people were naturally attracted
& easily caught the fire; Soon
after this we started services of
a revival character in our
large Mission Room at Gorsenion,
night after night the people
thronged together & we gave
portions of the service and an

address & then threw the meeting
open — the people readily & spontaneously
took part, and the Clergyman in
charge of the service would walk
up & down the aisle exhorting the
people: & many from time to
time acknowledged the Saviour as
their King. Then at Pontardulais we
had the parish Church restored &
had our re-opening services on the
10th November; & it was on the 13th
& 14th Nov: the people were visibly
affected — there was not a single
dry eye in the Church. No revival
service had been held then in
Pontardulais. And many nonconformists who were present
on the 14th Nov: speak of that

Place	Converts
Aberaman	510
Aberavon	325
Aberbeeg	206
Abercarn	380
Abercrave	83
Abercwmboy	156
Abercynon	720
Aberdare	728
Abergwynfi and Blaengwynfi	480
Aberkenfig	266
Abernant	104
Abersychan, Pontnewynydd, Talywain, Garndiffaith, and Varteg	455
Abertillery, Sixbells, and Cwmtillery	3,487
Abertridwr	124
Aberystwyth and district	220
Ammanford	319
Barry	676
Bargoed	191
Beaufort	238
Bedlinog	190
Bodwas	50
Bettws	15
Birchgrove	33
Blackwood	368
Blaenavon	1,200
Blaengarw	585
Blaenpennal	15
Blaina	1,069
Bontnewydd (near St. Asaph)	15
Brecon	51
Bridgend	307
Briton Ferry	408
Bryncethin and District	145
Brynmawr	466
Bryn (Port Talbot)	70
Llanelly, Loughor, and Felinfoel	1,758
Llanelly Hill (Brecon)	90
Llangattock	53
Llangeitho	45
Llangamarch	20
Llangennech	86
Llangyfelach	24
Llanharan	245
Llanhilleth	261
Llanishen	17
Llannon	11
Llanstephan	
Llawhaden (Pem.)	5
Llantwit Major	145
Llwydcoed	85
Llwynhendy	170
Llwynpiod	
Llwynypia	21
Machen	
Maesteg and district	2,09?
Maenclochog	
Maesycwmmer	1
Maindee (Newport)	6?
Mardy	94
Merthyr	
Merthyr Vale	81
Michaelstone	
Middle Hill (Haverfordwest)	106
Milford Haven	12
Miskin	
Morriston	1,666
Mountain Ash	1,050
Mynyddbach	14
Nantymoel	359
Nantyglo	501
Narberth	
Neath	1,538
Neath Abbey	92
Nelson	385
Newbridge	500
New Quay	350
(Pem.)	23
Builth Wells and district	216
Burry Port	350
Bwlchyllan	20
Caerau	57
Caerphilly	570
Capcoch	51
Cardiff	2,753
Cardigan and district	55
Carmarthen	512
Cefncribbwr	75
Cefngarnydd	7
Cilfrew and Coynant	122
Cilfynydd	721
Clydach (Brecon)	70
Clydach-on-Tawe	200
Clydach Vale	850
Coedpoeth	70
Coity	24
Cowbridge	28
Coychurch, Trecs, and Llangan	70
Crickhowell	156
Crosshands and Tumble	339
Crosskeys	500
Crumlin	18
Crynant	85
Cwmaman	670
Cwmamman (Carm.)	559
Cwmavon (Port Talbot)	800
Cwmbach	402
Cwmbran	189
Cwmdare	94
Cwmgwrach	141
Cwmllynfell	130
Cwmpark and Brithdir	135
Cymmer	79
Dinas	64
Dowlais and Penydarren	1,365
Drayton	10
Drefach and Velindre	89
Ebbw Vale	1,720
Ferndale and Blaen-	
New Tredegar	
New Milford	300
New Inn (Pontypool)	88
Ogmore Vale	360
Pembrey and Pwll	163
Pembroke	70
Pembroke Dock	150
Penarth	400
Penclawdd	193
Pencoed	150
Penderyn (Aberdare)	10
Penrhiwceiber	597
Pentre	1,304
Penywaun (Aberdare)	50
Peterstone	15
Pentyrch	11
Penygraig	749
Penyfae	25
Pontardawe	212
Pontardulais	435
Pontlottyn	242
Pontnewydd	62
Pontrhydfendigaid	110
Pontrhydyfen	75
Pontrhydygroes	20
Pontyberem	150
Pontyclun and district	120
Pontycymmer	971
Pontygwaith	351
Pontypool	457
Pontypridd	1,389
Pontyrhyl	92
Porth	658
Porthcawl	49
Pumpsaint (Car.)	211
Resolven	702
Reynoldston (Pem.)	30
Rhayader	100
Rhuddlan	13
Rhymney	868
Risca	854
Robertstown	67
Rogerstone	450
Rudry	50
St. Bride's	29
St. Clears	66
St. David's	36
St. Vaun's	60

< Newspaper list of converts

that locality some twelve years ago with a membership of eleven—now 180 strong, with an average Sunday school attendance of 220. After the great success of the revival, it was decided to greatly increase the proposed new building, and provision will be made in the church for 700 and in the schoolroom underneath for 400. Mr. David Davies, Llandinam, now M.P. for Montgomeryshire, laid the first stone on December 15th, and contributed £100 to the building fund.

Another phenomenal increase of membership, calling for increased accommodation, was that of Nebo Baptist Chapel, Ebbw Vale. During the revival 180 converts were received into full membership by the Rev. J. A. Evans, making a total of nearly 400, compared with 130 twelve years ago, and Sunday school scholars to the number of 300, as against 80 twelve years since. Old Nebo Chapel was built in 1825, from which sprang several branches. In the nineties a more convenient site was secured, and an iron erection put up at a cost of £700, which is cleared off in seven years. The new building is upon the site of the former iron structure, and will afford accommodation for 700 in the chapel and 300 in the schoolroom, the whole being designed for future extension in the way of classrooms, organ chamber, &c.

The Monmouthshire Congregational Union are raising £1,000 for building extensions throughout the county, and other bodies are also taking steps to provide for wants of a similar character. In fact, there are few places of worship which have not undergone some alteration or have some improvement scheme in hand, if perhaps on a smaller scale to the cases quoted above.

NEWPORT AND DISTRICT.

Mr Evan Roberts did not visit Newport, but Mr Sidney Evans and others held a series of meetings in the district, and the effects of the efforts then put forth are still felt in the religious and social life of the town. It is computed that as a result of the missions held by Mr George Clarke, Mr Sidney Evans, and others at the time of the revival fully 1,000 converts were registered in Newport alone. Careful inquiries show that about 15 per cent. of these have fallen off, and the remarkable feature is that the falling off has pro rata been more marked in the English than in the Welsh churches. It is difficult to explain this, for the English churches as a whole nobly rose to the occasion, and made special efforts to conserve the good results secured. The revival undoubtedly swept away a good deal of sectarian prejudice in the town, not only among the Free Churches, but as between the latter and the Anglican Churches. Evidence of this is the fact that the other day the clergymen and ministers of all denominations and presidents of various religious and social institutions issued a joint appeal to the electors in favour of giving more power to the Corporation to suppress the betting evil. The appeal was not so successful as it might have been, nevertheless it indicates that a step forward has been made by way of uniting the churches. Had it not been for the joint effort of the churches and other organisations the bookmakers would proba...

...tions issued a joint appeal to the electors in favour of giving more power to the Corporation to suppress the betting evil. The appeal was not so successful as it might have been, nevertheless it indicates that a step forward has been made by way of uniting the churches. Had it not been for the joint effort of the churches and other organisations the bookmakers would probably have been successful in defeating the Corporation proposals.

The Inrush of Converts.

There are other evidences that the revival gave a big impetus to the religious life of the town. Churches and mission-rooms are springing up on all sides. Once waning causes are now vigorous, and churches have been inspired to go forward. The Forward Movement had decided upon erecting a new hall before the revival started, but the inrush of 200 converts has led them to make their central hall much larger than was originally intended. The Malpas-road branch of the Forward Movement have decided to purchase the freehold of their hall, and at Corporation-road a new institute has been opened right in the centre of "Lysaght's Colony." To this institute the sheetworkers are flocking in large numbers. The Newport and District Presbyterians are also erecting a new schoolroom at Cross Hands, and it is expected that this will be opened in about six weeks' time.

Likewise the Baptists of the town are forging ahead. The small cause at Llanthewy-road is now vigorous, with a minister of its own. The Alma-street Baptist Church also had a small place of worship in Alexandra-road, but this came to grief, and the chapel was offered for sale at the Westgate Hotel. One of the enthusiasts arranged terms to take over the building, and to-day the church is likely to hold its own. The Summerhill Baptists have erected an iron church on Corporation-road, which is giving a good account of itself.

The Congregationalists, United Free Methodists, and Wesleyans may not have progressed so much by way of new buildings, but they have retained a substantial number of their converts. The meetings at all the churches are also characterised by the fact that the young people now take an active part in church work.

The Anglican Church has not been behind by way of converts and in conducting open-air missions. The Clewer Sisterhood—an organisation in connection with St John the Baptist Church—has for years been doing good work at the home in Severn-terrace in rescuing young girls from undesirable influences and maintaining and training them for service. For this work new premises are now to be erected in Oakfield-road, off Risca-road. The new buildings will cost £14,000, and over £9,000 has already been promised in subscriptions.

All this is having a material effect on the morals of the town. The police court records — particularly of drunkenness — for the past year show a diminution in the number of cases.

BRUTAL BRUSSELS MURDER.

SW/Feb 14

1906.

The Revival---and After.

RESULTS IN MONMOUTHSHIRE.

CHURCH EXTENSIONS ON ALL HANDS.

The Monmouthshire Western Valley districts generally benefitted greatly from the revival of 1904-5. Apart from the innumerable personal testimonies to the lasting character of the wonders worked during that time there have also arisen several worthy monuments in "bricks and mortar," to say nothing of the many agencies set in operation for the social welfare of the community. Here, as elsewhere, there has been experienced a falling off in the number of converts, but the general opinion expressed is that the many—and they are numerous—who have remained faithful to their professions have maintained an almost unhoped-for fidelity. Not only so, but the Sunday services, together with the week night prayer, temperance, Bible class, and other meetings, are attended by old members as well as new as they had never been before. In innumerable instances additions and alterations have been effected, or are in contemplation, by churches—increased Sunday school and sitting accommodation, the provision of musical instruments, &c., according to the particular needs of the places of worship concerned, but one or two cases may be particularly cited as standing out prominently. For instance, there is the experience of the Blaenau Gwent Baptist Church, Abertillery. The pastor, the Rev. T. T. Evans, took an active part in the revival movement, during which the actual membership of the church increased from 400 to nearly 800. As a result the old chapel was soon found too small to "house" the new members, and it was decided that a new church should be erected to accommodate 1,200 at a cost of £4,200. In July last Mr Richard Cory, J.P., of Cardiff, laid the foundation stone, and the undertaking was started with the heartiest congratulations. Last year, too, Ebenezer Baptist Church, Abertillery, opened Sunday school buildings comprising many well-arranged, serviceable class rooms, at a cost of over £2,000; similar provision has also been made by the English Baptists at Abercarn, and Ebenezer, Llanhilleth, has also a new building scheme in hand at the present time.

At Abertillery the Wesleyan Methodist body have also in hand a scheme for re-building. The present chapel was built in 1851 and has...

Attack on the 'Evan Roberts' Revival

< The Rev Peter Price

< Evan Roberts

Not everyone was pleased with Evan Roberts' methods. The most prominent attack was by the Rev Peter Price at the end of January 1905. The attack led to days of letters being printed for and against the Revivalists' methods in the *Western Mail*. Evan Roberts did not reply or retaliate to any of the criticisms.

[handwritten: W. M. Jwrott Jay 31]

tant teachers, however, stand in the line of least resistance, and they have to suffer. The assistant teachers, however, stand together loyally, declining the proffered terms, because they detest persecution of this sort. We hope the people of Barry are proud of their district council.

ONE OR TWO REVIVALS?

To-day we publish an article on the Revival and Mr. Evan Roberts which must prove painful reading to many thousands of our readers. It is written by the Rev. Peter Price, of Dowlais, a prominent Nonconformist minister, whose attitude towards Mr. Evan Roberts and the movement of which, as we believe, he is the human mainspring is one of uncompromising opposition. Mr. Price starts the curiously strange theory that we have in Wales, not one, but two Revivals, the one true and Heaven-born, the other false and—well, born of Mr. Evan Roberts. Now, it is well that our readers should clearly bear in mind that Mr. Price makes no attempt to prove that there is a Revival in Wales distinct and apart from that with which Mr. Evan Roberts is identified. His object, however, is not so much to prove his assertion make an unwarrantable attack upon Mr. Evan Roberts, for reasons which are best known, of course, to its author. It is absolutely incorrect to say that there was a Revival movement in Wales prior to the meetings which Mr. Roberts and his friends held at Loughor. That there

DOUBLE REVIVAL IN WALES.

A STRANGE ATTACK ON MR. EVAN ROBERTS.

By the Rev. PETER PRICE, B.A.
[Congregational Minister at Dowlais.]

We publish the following article, from the pen of a prominent Congregationalist minister, because, if the opinions of the writer are held by many, it is right that they should be expressed in order that they may be met by those who believe, as we do, that Mr. Evan Roberts is the human mainspring of the religious movement which has produced such remarkable results in Wales during the past three months. The subject is dealt with in our leading article.—ED.

I write the following in the interest of the religion of Jesus Christ, and because I sympathise with visitors who come from long distances "to see the Revival" in South Wales.

Now, I think I can claim that I have had as good an opportunity as most people to understand what is really going on in South Wales; and I have come to the conclusion that there are two so-called Revivals going on amongst us. The one, undoubtedly, from above—Divine, real, intense in its nature, and Cymric in its form. It is almost an impossibility for strangers who know not our temperament, nor our language, nor our religious history, to understand this. Their best method would be to go unannounced to some of our Sunday or week-day services, and, if possible, to remain unrecognised. Here they might

proved himself so a prophecy concerning certain "misgivings" of his as to whether he ought to have undertaken a mission to Dowlais!

I should like to ask Evan Roberts a few questions—I have many more which I might ask, but I will be satisfied now with a few:—

1. He said that there was someone in the lobby who was accepting Christ, but no one did. What spirit told him this lie?

2. When requested to speak in English he has repeatedly said that he is not prompted by the Spirit, and that when thus prompted he would do so. Why did he not tell the straight truth and say, "I don't know English," which I am told is the fact? And what about the Spirit on the day of Pentecost? Has He changed?

3. Why does he wait until the meetings attain the climax of enthusiasm before he enters? If help is valuable at any stage, is it not mostly so at the commencement in order to kindle the fire?

4. Why does he visit places where the fire has been burning at maximum strength for weeks and months? Would it not be more reasonable for him to go to places which the fire has not reached?

5. What spirit makes him bad-tempered when things don't come about exactly as he wishes?

6. What spirit makes him say, "Ask God to damn the people if you don't ask anything else?

Yes, but he has a lovely face and a beautiful smile—so some women say. This is the last resort.

May I repeat that I have written the above in the interest of the religion of Jesus Christ, and out of sympathy with visitors who come "to see the Revival." I may have to suffer persecution for writing the above—even by "spirit-filled" men (!), but I don't seek the renown of

---

Part of the article attacking Evan Roberts in the Western Mail

Dear Friend - God loves you therfore seek him diligently: pray to him earnestly, read his word constantly, Yours in the gospel Evan Roberts /

Dear Friend - God loves you

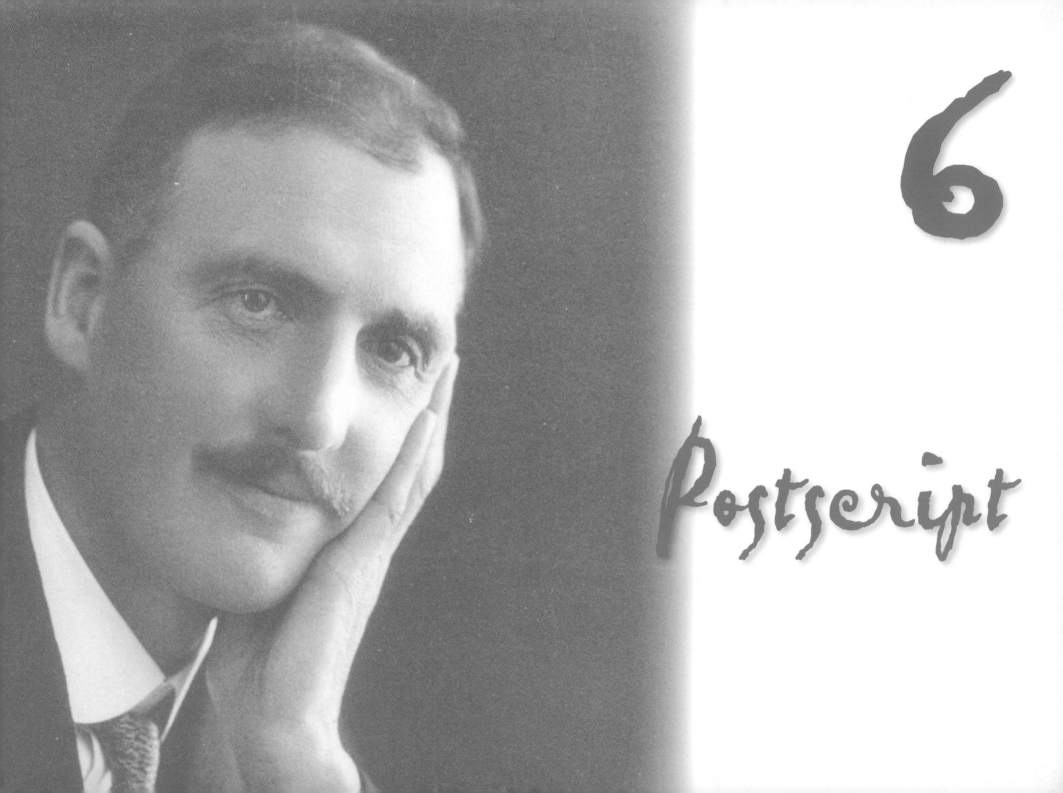

6

Postscript

< Great Glen, Leicester, the house where Evan Roberts stayed after the Revival.

War on the Saints

A Text Book for believers on the work of deceiving spirits among the children of God

By Mrs. PENN-LEWIS

in collaboration with

EVAN ROBERTS

< Evan Roberts in his thirties

After the Revival, Evan Roberts went to recuperate at the home of Mr and Mrs Jessie Penn-Lewis at Leicester. Due to the strain of the Revival services, the process took months. Advised not to engage in any more public ministry, he devoted himself to intercessory prayer and writing. He eventually returned to Wales in the mid 20s and was involved in a series of prayer meetings at a place called Gorseinon where many were reminded of the Revival days. From 1930 to his death he lived quietly in Cardiff, expressing himself increasingly through his poetry, most of which is still unpublished.

Flowers presented to the little girl who had been in the first Revival meeting

< Notice of the death of Evan Roberts

> PRICE.—On Jan. 28, at 2, Brynhyfryd, Tonypandy, Hannah, beloved wife of the late John Price, Contractor, in her 85th year, Funeral on Thursday, Feb. 1, at 11 o'clock, for Trealaw Cemetery.
ROBERTS.—Evan (the Welsh Revivalist 1904/5), on Jan. 29, at Cardiff. Funeral Thursday, Feb. 1, at 3 p.m., Moriah Chapel, Loughor. Friends please meet at Moriah Chapel.   1
ROSSI.—On Saturday, Jan 27, at 34, Bridge-st., Troedyrhiw, Luigi. Funeral Tuesday, 2.30 p.m., for Cefn Cemetery; private.
SAMWAYS.—On Jan. 29, at Ednyfed, Llandebie, Sarah Jane (wife of the late Herbert Samways, Headmaster, Maesybont School), aged 85. Funeral Thursday, Feb. 1, for Llanlluan Maesybont; private at house, public at Llanlluan, Maesybont, 2.30 p.m. No flowers.   1
SKINNER.—On Jan. 29, at 7, St. Fagans-ave., Barry, George William James, dearly-beloved husband of Ellen Maria and loving

∧ Obituary of Evan Roberts

< Evan Roberts in his sixties

v Evan Roberts' own words in a facsimile of his own hand on the Loughor Monument

> Dear Friend –
> God Loves you . Therefore, Seek Him
> diligently; Pray to Him earnestly
>
> Read His Word constantly.
>
> Yours in the Gospel
> Evan Roberts.

REMEMBER JESUS CHRIST.

The Revival Memorial Monument in front of Moriah Chapel, Loughor. The Rev and Mrs Sidney Evans **>**

COLOFN COFFA

1904 DIWYGIAD 1905

A'R

DIWYGIWR

EVAN ROBERTS

1879 1951

GWR DUW A CAIR DUW

Memorial at Moriah Chapel

PHOTOGRAPHIC ACKNOWLEDGEMENTS

Page	Subject	Source	Publisher/Collection
11	Newcastle Emlyn Castle	Emyr Jones	1904 Ltd
12	Statue of St David	Emyr Jones	1904 Ltd
12	St David's Cathedral	Emyr Jones	1904 Ltd
13	St Govan's Church	Gaynor Jones	1904 Ltd
13	St Govan's Detail	Gaynor Jones	1904 Ltd
14	Nevern Celtic cross	Emyr Jones	1904 Ltd
14	Nevern Celtic cross detail	Emyr Jones	1904 Ltd
15	Cenarth Falls	Gaynor Jones	1904 Ltd
15	Cenarth Mill	Gaynor Jones	1904 Ltd
16	Margam Abbey Print	Gastineux 1830s	Kevin Adams Personal Collection
17	Haverfordwest Abbey	Emyr Jones	1904 Ltd
17	Haverfordwest Abbey	Emyr Jones	1904 Ltd
18	King Henry VIII	History of Protestantism – J. A. Wylie	Casswell Petter & Galpin C19th
19	Martyrdom of Dr Farrar	Hanes Y Merthyron – Thomas Jones	T Gee A'I Fab (C1893)
20	Cannwyll Y Cymru	Cannwyll Y Cymru – Rees Pritchard	C18th copy no date.
20	The Morning Star	The Morning Star – Rees Pritchard	London 1785
21	Griffith Jones teaching	The Story of Carmarthenshire – D. Morgan	Educational Pub Co – Trade Street Cardiff
21	Griffith Jones Catechism Book pages	Esponiad Byr ar Gatecism yr Eglwys	London 1778
22	Hywel Harris	Y Tadau Methodistaidd – J.M. Jones	Swansea (1895)
22	George Whitefield	Early 19th Century Print	Kevin Adams Personal Collection
22	Daniel Rowland	Deuddeg Pregeth – Daniel Rowland	Dolgellau 1876
22	William Williams	Y Tadau Methodistaidd	Swansea 1895
23	Christmas Evans	C19th print	Kevin Adams Personal Collection
23	Thomas Charles	Y Tadau Methodistaidd	Swansea 1895
23	Williams from the Wern	Diwygiadau Crefyddol Cymru – Hughes	Caernarfon 1906
24	John Elias preaching	Lithograph of a painting by T.H.Thomas	National Library of Wales
24	John Elias	Enwogion Y Ffydd – Gol John Peter	London C19th
25	Bethania	Emyr Jones	1904 Ltd
25	4 Denominations in 1830	Diwygwyr Cymru – B.G. Evans	Author 1900
26	Maesyronnen Chapel	Y Tadau Methodistaidd	Swansea (1895)
26	Park Street Chapel	Postcard	John Hunter Collection
26	Tabernacle Llanelli	Postcard	John Hunter Collection
27	Bethlehem	Emyr Jones	1904 Ltd
27	Bethlehem	Emyr Jones	1904 Ltd
27	Bethlehem	Emyr Jones	1904 Ltd
27	Bethlehem	Emyr Jones	1904 Ltd
28	David Morgan	Humphrey Jones a Diwygiad 1859 E. Issac	Bala 1930
28	Humphrey Jones	Diwygiadau Crefyddol Cymru – Hughes	Caernafon 1906
29	Cynddylan Jones	Y Darluniadur 1900 – W. Lewis	Cardiff 1900
29	David Adams	David Adams by K. Evans	Liverpool 1924
31	Tabernacle New Quay	Life Story of Evan Roberts – Hicks	London 1905.
32	W S Jones	Postcard	Kevin Adams Personal Collection
32	Penuel, Carmarthen	History of Penuel	Emyr Jones Personal Collection
32	W W Lewis	Living Echoes – R. Ellis	The Delyn Press
32	Keri Evans	Living Echoes – R. Ellis	The Delyn Press
33	Carmarthen New	Huw Priday	1904 Ltd
33	Carmarthen New	Huw Priday	1904 Ltd
34	F. B. Meyer	Postcard	Kevin Adams Personal Collection
34	R.B. Jones	Postcard	Brynmor Jones Collection
35	Plaque of Dean Howell	Emyr Jones	1904 Ltd
35	Dean Howell	Welsh Religious Leaders – V. Morgan	London 1905
36	Seth Joshua	Life Story of Evan Roberts – Hicks	London 1905
37	New Quay Modern	Huw Priday	1904 Ltd
38	Tabernacle New Quay	Life Story of Evan Roberts – Hicks	London 1905
39	Joseph Jenkins	Life Story of Evan Roberts – Hicks	London 1905
39	Maude Davies and Florrie	Y Diwygiad a'r Diwygwyr	Dolgellau 1906
40	Florrie Evans	Life Story of Evan Roberts – Hicks	London 1905
40	May Phillips	Y Diwygiad a'r Diwygwyr	Dolgellau 1906
41	Tabernacle New Quay	Huw Priday	1904 Ltd
43	Evan Roberts	Evan Roberts A'I Waith – D.M. Phillips	Cardiff 1923
44	Evan Roberts	Evan Roberts A'I Waith – D.M. Phillips	Cardiff 1923
45	Henry Roberts	Y Diwygiad a'r Diwygwyr	Dolgellau 1906
45	Hannah Roberts	Moriah Chapel Photograph	Moriah Chapel Loughoir
45	Island House	Sunday Strand magazine	Desmond Cartwright Collection
46	Loughor Modern	Paul Griffiths	1904 Ltd
46	Loughor Modern	Paul Griffiths	1904 Ltd
46	Loghor Old	Postcard	John Hunter Collection
47	Traum	Coal Mining by Henry Davies	Welsh Educational Publishing Co (1904)
47	Man and Boy	Coal Mining by Henry Davies	Welsh Educational Publishing Co (1904)
47	Underground	Coal Mining by Henry Davies	Welsh Educational Publishing Co (1904)
48	Pit Head	Coal Mining by Henry Davies	Welsh Educational Publishing Co (1904)
48	Pit Head	Coal Mining by Henry Davies	Welsh Educational Publishing Co (1904)
48	Miners lamps	Coal Mining by Henry Davies	Welsh Educational Publishing Co (1904)
49	Miners	Coal Mining by Henry Davies	Welsh Educational Publishing Co (1904)
49	Mines Rescue	Coal Mining by Henry Davies	Welsh Educational Publishing Co (1904)
49	Explosion	Coal Mining by Henry Davies	Welsh Educational Publishing Co (1904)

A Diary of Revival > Kevin Adams

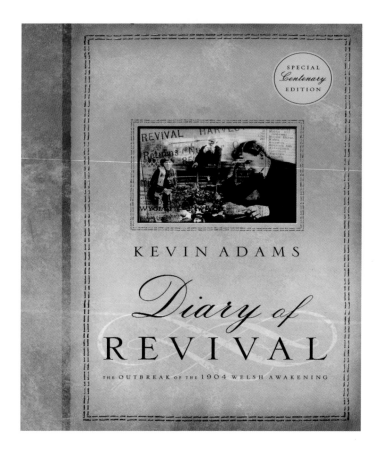

160 pages
Price: $14.99
ISBN: 0-8054-3195-0

A *Diary of Revival* contains extracts from the actual diaries of the revivalist Evan Roberts chronicling the events as the Revival broke. Many of these writings have never before been published and give a unique insight into what has been called the greatest move of God's Spirit in the last century.

· Actual diary notes as written by Evan Roberts and his contemporaries

· Pictures of churches, news reports and original church service sheets

· Trace the emergence of other ministries from the Revival

· Written by a leading authority on the 1904 awakening